W9-CMO-035

INTERIOR COLOR
BY DESIGN

VOLUME 2

A Tool for Homeowners, Designers, and Architects

ROCKPORT PUBLISHERS

JONATHAN POORE

PHOTOGRAPHS BY ERIC ROTH

© 2005 by Rockport Publishers, Inc.

All rights reserved. No part of this book may be reproduced in any form without written permission of the copyright owners. All images in this book have been reproduced with the knowledge and prior consent of the artists concerned and no responsibility is accepted by producer, publisher, or printer for any infringement of copyright or otherwise, arising from the contents of this publication. Every effort has been made to ensure that credits accurately comply with information supplied.

First published in the United States of America by
Rockport Publishers, Inc.
33 Commercial Street
Gloucester, Massachusetts 01930-5089
Telephone: (978) 282-9590
Fax: (978) 283-2742
www.rockpub.com

Control Number: 95198081

ISBN 1-59253-072-9

10 9 8 7 6 5 4 3 2 1

Design: Yee Design
Illustrations by Jonathan Poore

Printed in China
Printed in Singapore

In memory of Richard Poore, Jr.

CONTENTS

INTRODUCTION

Over the years, many people have asked me to create color schemes for various purposes. The more I do this type of work, the more I have come to realize that the most successful process does not really consist of me creating a color scheme for the client. The word *create* suggests that the color scheme springs from the creator's imagination. This surely does not describe the process adequately. It is more like helping someone learn a language so that he or she can find his or her own voice. The activity consists of learning about that individual and working together to draw out his or her unique color sensibilities.

When we step back to look at what was created at the conclusion of a color-consulting session, we often see the chosen palettes harmonize seamlessly with the individual's belongings, wardrobe, hair color, skin tone, and, in a fuller sense, the color of his or her personality and being. The palettes become a projection or extension of that unique individual. The fascinating thing is this personal color harmonizing is never a conscious process. We never set out to copy someone's personal color palette. It always grows out of dialogue about overall goals and preferences coupled with the constraints and opportunities of the existing living space.

I am often asked in what style I design or what my favorite styles are. I would have to say that I aspire to have no particular style at all. My design approach is more a facilitation process with the goal of helping people find the confidence to express themselves through the color and design of their personal environments. When I am asked to be a tastemaker, so to speak, I often draw a blank. For me, that is like trying to work in a vacuum. Seeking the richness of each individual's color sensibilities and helping him or her express these sensibilities is the "style" I strive for.

BUILDING YOUR COLOR CONFIDENCE

A comment I often hear from my clients is, "I love color, but I have no ability to select color." Another comment is, "I don't know how to select color, but I know what I like." If these statements ring true with your own experience, you have the awareness and sensitivity to work successfully with color. What you need is some simple tools to organize your process.

My most satisfying experiences in color consulting occur when, after a few sessions—where I do most of the talking and asking of questions—I start to feel the balance shift toward the client doing the work with me merely coaching from the sidelines. In one large project, featured in this book, after a few long, intense color sessions I just showed up with my color samples, sat back, and let the client do all the selecting. The client had no prior training or experience but waded right into the process with amazing skill and creativity.

At times, the empowering qualities of the process are palpable. In one instance, I did some color consulting with a young woman who had little confidence in her aesthetic decisions. She still lived with her parents and relied on them to make most decisions for her. Initially, she resisted even having a dialogue about color in her environment. I encouraged her to take an active role in choosing her own color palette for her private spaces. I showed her some methods, which helped her to trust her aesthetic judgment and make the color decisions on her own. She gradually found her color voice and was thrilled to exercise some control over her environment in such a simple, fun, but dramatic way. At the outset, she was hesitant to even express an opinion. By the end of the process, she was full of enthusiasm and ready for another color task.

BUT THE CHOICES ARE OVERWHELMING

I frequently hear people say, "I can tell what color combinations I like when I see them but am overwhelmed by all the choices." By laying out a step-by-step process to follow in color selection, you can simplify the process without inadvertently creating a simplistic result. I have had an opportunity to work with a number of people who have described themselves as having varying degrees of difficulty organizing and prioritizing their thoughts and tasks. The common characteristic these people shared was difficulty making decisions when presented with a wide array of choices. Selecting colors is one of those activities where the choices seem endless and all choices appear to have similar merit.

I have seen these clients, who tell me they suffer from decision-making difficulties, achieve tremendous success by going through an easy-to-follow progression of choices. They make their color decisions quickly and painlessly. More important, they remain committed to these color decisions through the completion of the project. Afterward, they tell me how elated they feel to have personally created a rich, colorful environment that is truly an extension of who they are.

No matter the level of your aesthetic decision-making skills, by using some easy-to-follow guidelines, you can learn the language of color and find confidence in your color voice. The language of color is a universal language, and people love to speak it.

HOW TO USE THIS BOOK

The primary goal of *Interior Color by Design*, Volume 2, is to equip the professional designer as well as the homeowner with the tools and understanding to use color effectively in architectural and interior design. It is designed to be used as a reference manual, an actual tool, to experiment with and design color schemes. Part I outlines the basics of color theory as they apply to interior design. Each principle of color theory is illustrated with specific examples of richly colored interiors to both explain the theory and spark the imagination. Part II, a virtual library of color ideas, is a compilation of sample color combinations. Each type of color scheme is shown in a sample interior and is followed with color chips showing variations on that color theme.

The greatest challenge in color design is to predict and control the result of a color scheme. Effective color selection can be an inexpensive, yet powerful, element in any design. Color can perform multiple roles and can affect a person's emotions, energy level, and sense of order—or disorder. In addition, it can set the tone of an interior and make it seem formal or informal, masculine or feminine, coolly aloof or invitingly warm. The aim of successful interior color design is to control these effects through the masterful use of color as a design tool itself. *Interior Color by Design,* Volume 2, outlines some basic techniques that take the mystery out of the color-design process.

Color design is not a science, but by becoming familiar with some basic rules of color theory, you can find a comfortable jumping-off point and apply the rules fairly literally to come up with conservative, but successful, color schemes. As your skill and confidence increases, you can take a more intuitive approach to color design, often bending the rules for more imaginative effects.

PART I

Chapter 1 Basic Color Theory

ATTRIBUTES OF COLOR

Hue or Color

The first attribute of color is **hue**, which is the name for a color, such as yellow, green, blue, and red. The color wheel is used to represent the basic colors (hues) of the visible spectrum. All the hues indicated on the color wheel are of full intensity. For the sake of simplicity, the most common color wheel comprises twelve color gradations, even though an infinite number of color gradations are possible between each color on the wheel.

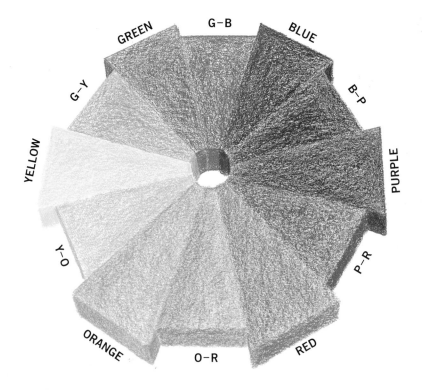

Figure 1.1 Color wheel

Value

The second attribute of color is **value** or the relative lightness or darkness of a color. Lighter values are achieved by adding white to a color, and darker values result from adding black.

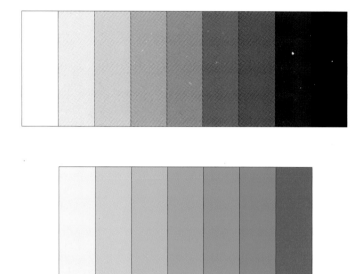

Figure 1.2 Gray value scale and green value scale

Chroma or Saturation

The third attribute of color is **chroma** or **saturation**. This attribute is the relative purity or intensity of a color, which is determined by how much or how little gray is added to it. The value of the colors on a chroma scale do not change; only the intensity of the color varies.

Figure 1.3 Green chroma scale

So, the three attributes of color—**hue, value,** and **chroma**—define every color. Color theorist Albert Munsell describes each and every color as having three dimensions; therefore, to fully describe any color it is necessary to describe each of these dimensions or attributes.

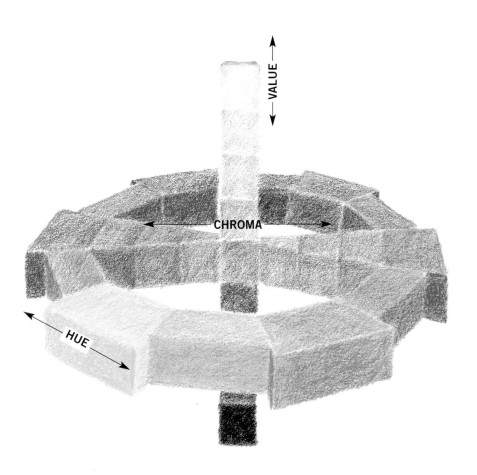

Figure 1.4 *Hue, value, and chroma—the three dimensions of color*

OTHER COLOR TERMS

Other color terms useful for a basic understanding of color theory are **tint, shade,** and **tone**. All of these are colors of full intensity or chroma mixed with white, black, or some value of gray.

- **Tint**—A color mixed with white (pastels)
- **Shade**—A color mixed with black
- **Tone**—A color mixed with some value of gray

FULL INTENSITY	TINT
FULL INTENSITY	**TINT**
SHADE	**TONE**

Figure 1.5 *Tint, shade, and tone of red*

COLOR TEMPERATURE

Colors are often referred to as either **warm** or **cool**. The colors on the color wheel are easy to separate into warm and cool colors. Red, orange, and yellow are considered warm, whereas green, blue, and purple are described as cool. As colors become less pure, the terms warm and cool become more useful as relative comparisons rather than absolute descriptions.

HOW COLORS MIX

Additive Color

Natural light contains all the colors of the spectrum. By breaking down light into its component parts, or spectral colors, it is possible to combine and mix the individual colors to form new ones. **Additive color** is the process of mixing colored light. The most common application of this can be found in theater lighting. For example, a red light overlapping a green light produces a yellow light. Colored pigments, however, behave differently than colored light when combined or mixed. The primary colors of light are red, green, and blue; the primary colors of pigments are red, yellow, and blue. When all three primary colors of light are combined, they form white light; when two colors of light are added together, they always produce a color of lighter value.

    The principles of additive color are most critical in theater or other dramatic lighting. For the purposes of interior color design, it is important to understand the effect of artificial lighting on the perception of color. For example, incandescent light brings out the warm colors of an interior whereas standard fluorescent light emphasizes the cool colors.

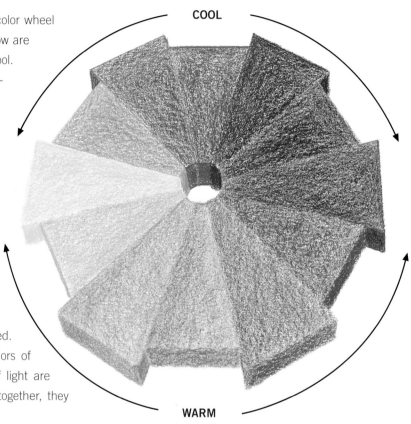

COOL

WARM

Figure 1.6 *Cool and warm colors*

Subtractive Color

Subtractive color is the result of mixing pigments, dyes, or other colorants. The apparent color of a surface is based on what part of the visible spectrum of light is absorbed versus what portion is reflected back to the viewer. Because the main concern of this book is the color of interior finishes—not lighting—the focus will be on subtractive rather than additive color.

The **primary** subtractive colors are red, yellow, and blue. These colors are called primary colors because all other colors are derived from some combination of these three. When all three primary colors are combined in equal amounts, the resulting color is a deep blackish brown. Note that the primary colors are spaced equidistant from one another on the color wheel. Midway between each primary color is a **secondary** color. When two adjacent primary colors are combined, they form the secondary color found between them on the color wheel. For example, yellow and blue paint mixed together make green. The other secondary colors are orange (red and yellow combined) and purple (red and blue combined). When adjacent primary and secondary colors are mixed, they form **tertiary** colors. Between each of the six primary and secondary colors are the tertiary colors, consisting of red-orange, orange-yellow, yellow-green, green-blue, blue-purple, and purple-red.

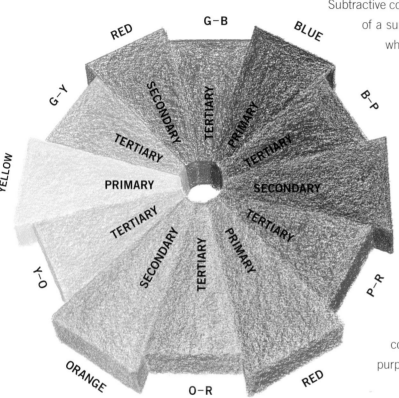

Figure 1.9 *Color wheel showing primary, secondary, and tertiary colors*

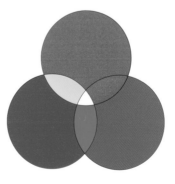

Figure 1.7 *Additive color*

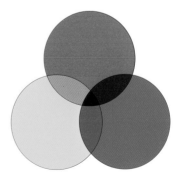

Figure 1.8 *Subtractive colors*

Partitive Color

When viewing a consistent, fine pattern of two distinct colors from a slight distance, the eye tends to perceive the colors as combined, which derives a third color. This is called **partitive** color. A commonly used example of partitive color is the post-Impressionist painting technique of pointillism, in which small dots or points of different colors are placed on the canvas to create an extremely rich, vibrant color. In architectural color, the greatest richness and depth is achieved with partitive color mixing, such as in glazing or in the stippling techniques of decorative painting. The subtle, multicolor effects of stone or wood are examples of partitive color as it appears in natural materials. When granite is viewed very closely, numerous shades of gray, black, and white are apparent, yet when viewed from a distance, all the specks of color blend to form a complex, rich gray that would be unachievable with a uniformly colored surface.

Partitive Color versus Flat Color Even though the color of the walls in each of these spaces is quite similar, the effect achieved is remarkably different. The rich purple color in the bathroom, opposite, is a result of a glazing technique. Rather than consisting of a single paint color, the wall color is composed of several layers of different colors. The base color, or underlying color, is considerably lighter than the deep glaze color or top color. Neither of the colors used in the glazing technique is remotely close to the single purple wall color of the sitting room below, yet when you look at the glazed wall, your eye blends the two colors in the glaze. In your mind you then perceive a third color that almost matches the single purple color of the sitting room.

Note that each of these rooms is extremely successful in its own right. The depth of the purple-glazed walls in the bathroom balances and complements the rich wood tones in the mirror frame. The main event in the sitting room is the exquisitely delicate and detailed paper figurines, which look dramatically three dimensional in contrast to the flatness of the dark purple wall.

Chapter 2 Architectural Considerations in Color Design

Setting the Emotional Tone *The rich, soft pink and wood tones in this bathroom create inviting and sensuous warmth in the room. The layering of colors and textures takes away any harsh, antiseptic qualities often associated with bathrooms.*

COLOR AS AN ARCHITECTURAL DESIGN INGREDIENT

Architectural and interior design consists of the manipulation of many interrelated elements, including space, form, structure, light, texture, and color. Unfortunately, the one ingredient in the interdependent mix of design elements that is most often overlooked or left as an afterthought is color. Color often sets the whole psychological tone and feel of a space. Because it is such a powerful ingredient in setting the character of an interior, it is well worth considering the overall color direction early in the design process. The best approach to color selection is to treat it as an integral part of the design rather than something that is applied superficially after the fact.

Effective color design does not need to add any cost to interior renovations or construction— it is a simple matter of planning ahead. The best strategy is to look at all the material colors and the paint colors as a single color composition in the service of your overall design goals. Is the space meant to be restful or lively? Should the interior create a neutral backdrop for the furnishings, or should it be a strong color statement in and of itself?

The most successful interior color design is responsive and appropriate to the overall design goals. The first step is to identify the design goals. Then, determine if color could be used to set a mood or could it be used as a problem solver to bolster the interior design. It is helpful at this stage to determine what elements of an interior design you want to play up or what elements you just want to blend in. Color is an extremely effective tool for drawing your attention to the desirable qualities of a space and camouflaging the problems in the space. Some of the other important roles color can play include:

- Setting the emotional tone or ambiance of a space
- Focusing or diverting attention
- Modulating the space to feel larger or smaller
- Breaking up and defining the space
- Unifying the space or knitting it together

ABOVE | *Setting the Ambience* The pale, cool colors in this dining room create a simple, clean, open atmospheric ambience. The warm accents keep the room from feeling too stark.

RIGHT | *Focusing Attention* One of the most dramatic design features in this formal living room is the gracefully vaulted ceiling. This space is used principally in the evening hours, so a dramatic midnight blue was incorporated to call attention to this unusual architectural feature and to create the effect of being under a canopy of night sky. The period paneling and trim work in this room is accented in five subtly different gradations of warm cream and gold tones. This subtle layering of colors on the paneling and trim gives the walls of the room enough mass or weight that they can visually carry the deep blue ceiling. Without this illusion of weight and substance in the walls, the dark ceiling would feel top heavy and unsettlingly intrusive.

LEFT | *Modulating Space to Feel Larger*
The ceiling in this kitchen is quite low, but the technique of painting both the walls and the ceilings in the same sunny, light-enhancing color creates the illusion that this space is much taller and grander. The overall monochromatic palette in the kitchen keeps the entire design clean and spacious looking.

LEFT | *Modulating Space to Feel More Intimate* *The red tint of the ceiling creates a soft, warm glow in this sitting area. The red color advances, making the ceiling feel lower and creating a sense of intimate enclosure.*

OPPOSITE | *Defining the Space* The intricate interplay of lines, planes, and geometric shapes in this dramatic living space would be lost without the use of color to differentiate the architectural forms. The horizontal bands of color wandering through the space give it scale and proportion. These bands also trace the various curves and architectural shapes. The sky dome has a graded wash of blues, which wander from pale to deep blue as they move away from the natural light sources. All the surfaces have various layers of colored glazes over them so the palette is constantly shifting from extremely subtle hints and blends of color to dramatically saturated accents. Note the subtle ochre, rust, and green highlights in the crown molding below the balcony rail. The color in this space is designed to maintain a constant dialogue between the spatial drama and the architectural nuances.

ABOVE | *Unifying the Space* The contrasting wood tones of all the trim work in this contemporary interior serve to create an organizing grid so the interior has a carefully balanced, decorative, geometric pattern. The wood tones are sensitively woven into the overall color palette so they are harmoniously integrated.

ABOVE | *Breaking Up and Defining Space* This bedroom space has a high ceiling and high windows. A simple technique to break up a large expanse of wall is to add a picture molding and create a color break. Doing so gives these otherwise small windows some context, organizes the room into more pleasing proportions, and, last but not least, creates an excuse to have a change of color. In this case the muted yellow and green combination is restful without being somber.

INTERACTIVENESS OF COLOR RELATIONSHIPS

Have you ever picked out a color independently from another color selection, only to find they clash when you put them together? You were sure you liked each of the colors by themselves, but together, you didn't like either one anymore—they didn't even look like the colors you originally chose. Colors cannot be selected without taking into account all the adjacent colors and materials in the space. This process requires examining the total environment in which the colors will be used. Adjacent colors can have a very strong effect on one another; therefore, it is important to be able to predict and control their interaction. By itself, a very muted color often looks absolutely neutral, yet when placed against a complementary muted color, both appear to come alive and be stronger colors. Color is so interactive that when it is placed in juxtaposition to another color or colors, the original color can appear to change hue, value, or saturation. The surest way to predict and control the color relationships in an interior is to get actual samples of the colors or materials and place them directly against the other colors in the space.

Understanding and mastering the art of color interaction, even in its most rudimentary form, gives you a powerful design tool. One of the most common errors in interior color design is selecting a single strong color for a space that then overpowers the room. Soon you will tire of living with the color. The problem is that by trying to set the tone in the room with a single color, you are forced to select a strong color. A single muted color looks bland, so you lean toward a more saturated, intense color. Then, when you actually see the space completely swathed in the color, it is too much.

ABOVE | *The cool gray cabinets in this kitchen are complemented by the warm white trim. Each of these colors on its own would appear neutral, yet when they are juxtaposed the effect is soft blue against warm cream. The warm wood tones add some weight and depth to the space.*

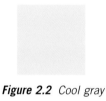

Figure 2.2 Cool gray

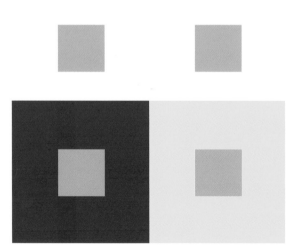

Figure 2.1 The same color against two different color backgrounds appears to change hue

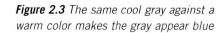

Figure 2.3 The same cool gray against a warm color makes the gray appear blue

Strong Color Relationships—
Not Strong Colors

When you select colors based on how they will interact with one another, you can easily select softer, more muted colors because the dynamic interplay of the colors is what creates the richness and visual interest. In certain instances, an intense color might be just the right choice, but the point here is for you to have control over the selection process so you can have a dynamic color scheme without being forced to use stronger colors than you want.

Color design is about creating a harmonious composition out of many different colors and design elements. It is about putting the pieces together in a unified way. One way to think about color design is to visualize the process as conducting orchestra musicians through a piece of music. Each musician has a specific role to play. Some are in leading roles, and some in supporting roles. As each musician performs, his or her music is layered on and juxtaposed against the next musician's. The overall harmony in the music is created from the interactions between all the musicians—it is a team effort. In your interior, if you select each color in isolation for its individual interest, then try to put them all together, it will be a lot like the orchestra conductor giving the instruction for everyone to solo at once. The result will be cacophony.

ABOVE | *The neutral gray room with neutral white trim has a museum-like sophistication. Without color contrasts or subtle complementary colors, this color scheme remains completely neutral as a backdrop for the black-and-white prints.*

HINT #1
Strong color relationships—
not strong colors

Select the intensity of a color based on how it looks with the adjacent colors rather than how interesting it looks by itself.

ABOVE | The warm white and cool gray play off each other to interactively create cream and blue. The perception that the cool gray appears blue is amplified by the juxtaposition of the blue and white china.

RIGHT | The dark green paint in this period room is rich with patina and character. By itself, the green color is so deep that it appears almost black, but the complementary, deep red accents in the space bring out the green color.

CONSIDERING CONTEXT

The context of your space is the launching point for all color decisions. Context ranges from the quality of the available natural light to the existing wood floor color. Responding to the context is what creates a fuller sense of harmony in the space. Ignoring the context creates aesthetic conflicts and causes you to miss wonderful design opportunities. For example, if a particular room has muted north light and you want it to have a bright, cheerful feeling, select clear, clean, warm, pastel colors or rich, full-saturation, warm colors rather than muted gray colors to avoid making the space look dull, flat, and gray.

The context consists of everything in the space that is a given, such as all the elements of the interior over which you have no control or to which you have already been committed. The most successful color schemes are responsive to these inherent characteristics of the space. Fully understanding the context of your space requires careful and sensitive observation. Analyzing context can even include awareness of and sensitivity to your region of the country. Every region has a different quality of light and often a particular cultural preference for certain palettes.

Regional Color

Every region of the country has a different flavor color palette. You would never say that the dominant architectural colors you see in Florida are the same as those in Maine, nor are those in Maine and Florida anything like the colors you experience in the Arizona desert. The specific environment in which you live influences your color preferences and palettes. Every region has its own unique color palette in nature. The colors of the vegetation, trees, rocks, soil, and even the color of the sky and the quality of light each day have an effect on the regional color palette. The crisp, clear, reflected light along the New England coast is very different from the soft, misty light in the mountains of the Pacific Northwest.

Often, without even realizing, you will find that you are keyed into the palette of your own region because it becomes, in a sense, a cultural bias. It is just part of your daily experience, a way of harmonizing, unconsciously, with your environment. If you want to gain deeper understanding and some control over the harmony in your color environment, though, it is important to develop a more keen awareness of color in your surroundings—including the colors in nature and the quality of natural light that surrounds you.

ABOVE | *The crisp white trim color emphasizes the inherent symmetry of the room. The matched white built-ins frame the space like bookends.*

Orientation

The orientation of a room or space has a strong effect on the quality of light and, therefore, how you perceive color in that environment. It is important to observe the changes of light throughout the day. Also, try to understand the seasonal variations in light before making color decisions.

Another crucial factor is the position a color will occupy within the room. If it is on the same wall as a window, it will tend to look darker and grayer, especially if the windows are on only one wall. As an experiment, take a large color swatch and hold it against a wall across from the windows. Next, take that same swatch and hold it against the window wall. The combination of the bright backlight from the window, plus the lack of direct light on the window wall makes the color look duller and grayer.

NORTH LIGHT

North light is diffuse and cooler. It tends to be more soft, even, and less dramatic. Colors gray down a bit and feel more muted. If your goal is to have a cheerful, sunny, active space, then choose warm colors in lighter values. Contrasting accent colors become more important to give the room some depth and dimension in north light. If your goal is a more quiet, restful, contemplative space, use cooler colors with warm accents. Full-bodied blues and blue-greens appear richer in cool north light. Check your color samples carefully in the actual ambient light of the room and be sure they don't gray out too much.

SOUTH LIGHT

South light is crisp and sharp, and it creates strong contrasts within the space. It is a warm light. The perception of color in a space lit by south light changes continually through the day and even through the seasons. South light tends to be dramatic with pronounced shadows and highlights. If you are trying to play up the sunny character of a south-facing space, muted, warm colors are best so that the colors are not too harsh. For example, a soft creamy, yellow or earthy ochre color will be easier to live with than a primary yellow.

A bright, south-facing space provides an excellent opportunity to use complex and subtle cool colors. For example, a muted blue-green-gray creates a restful space that is constantly, but slightly, changing with the light. A color such as this is much like a chameleon. It appears to shift color, depending on the changing light and in response the accent colors next to it.

ABOVE | *The play of light on the different planes of the yellow walls is quite dramatic. The walls in the same plane as the windows appear darker and grayer than the walls that receive direct light from the window. When selecting colors, it is essential to view color samples in all the various natural-light orientations in which the colors will be seen. In this case, you would hold a swatch to the window wall and then hold the same swatch to the adjacent walls.*

OPPOSITE | *The full light in this space allows this muted, cool blue to still feel rich and inviting. The overall blue tonality of the room is quiet and restful, but the warm, off-white accents and the strongly contrasting patterns give the room a lively balance.*

EAST LIGHT AND WEST LIGHT

It can be a challenge to select colors for a space that has only east or west light. It is helpful to decide if the space is to be used principally in the morning or the afternoon. This way you can tailor the color selection to the type of light you will most often experience. East- or west-facing spaces are filled with dramatic light in the morning or afternoon, respectively. The sun enters at a low angle and penetrates deeply into the interior of the room. At certain times of day, an east- or west-facing space can be even brighter than a room with a south orientation. At other times of day, the room will be more similar to a north-facing space with cool, diffuse light.

For a balanced color scheme that works at all times of day, a simple, safe rule of thumb is to use muted warm colors with rich, cool accents. A rule of thumb is a safe jumping-off point in color design, but as you increase your confidence, try to bend, stretch, and eventually break the rules for truly inspirational solutions.

BELOW | *The rich terra-cotta glaze on the wall behind the sofa creates a cozy backdrop for this sitting area. The orientation of the room allows the natural light to penetrate deeply into the space and enrich the depth of color on the terra-cotta accent wall.*

The Proportions and Shape of Your Space

Every space has its own characteristic shape and proportions. Color can be used to play up the positive aspects of a space, such as calling attention to a soaring cathedral ceiling. Color can also enhance the classical proportions and symmetry of a period interior by highlighting the moldings and architectural details. By choosing a softly blended palette, color can organize and calm a room that is otherwise visually chaotic.

Color is also a versatile, inexpensive problem solver and can be used to downplay less desirable aspects of a room, such as a low ceiling. For example, by reducing the color and value contrast between the wall and ceiling plane, it is possible to blur the division between wall and ceiling, creating the illusion of a higher ceiling. Also a pale, cool tint of blue on a ceiling recedes and makes the ceiling appear to float ethereally above the walls like a soft sky canopy.

ABOVE | *This loft is defined by a series of partitions that occupy the space like freestanding sculptures. This sculptural effect is emphasized with a different color on each partition. This is often referred to as a volumetric use of color. In this case, the colors call out each partition as an individual volume.*

ABOVE | *This ceiling is a flat plane, but the shades of green and pale blue-green create the illusion that the ceiling is vaulted. This effect is possible because the cooler lighter blue shades recede while the warmer greens seem nearer.*

RIGHT | *The tall, narrow cathedral ceiling would most likely be unnoticed if not for the vibrant yellow drawing your eye up through this whimsical surprise of a space.*

LEFT | *The warmer and deeper colors of the walls contrast with the pale, cool blue of the ceiling in this vaulted living room. The blue tends to recede and make the vaulted ceiling seem even higher and more dramatic.*

ABOVE | *The deep, warm tone of the cathedral ceiling in this bedroom creates a sense of cozy intimacy. The yellow gold tone on the ceiling advances, making the ceiling seem lower than it actually is, which creates a more intimate scale without taking away from the spacious qualities of the room.*

ABOVE | **Bringing the Outside In** *The interior colors of this sunroom are carefully coordinated to harmonize with the exterior paint colors visible through the windows. The exterior colors are then woven into the colors of the natural landscape. The result is a continuity of color harmony from interior to exterior that truly creates an integrated suite of spaces. It brings the outside in and creates an overall sense of spaciousness.*

Think in Suites

Whenever you consider color in an interior space, it is essential to consider the particular space in the context of the whole interior. Unless you are confronted with a virtual maze of individual rooms, you can usually see from room to room in a single view. Often, in open-plan configurations, it is possible to see many different rooms simultaneously. In situations like this the importance of conceiving the color palettes in the context of the entire interior is obvious because you see all the colors in immediate juxtaposition to one another. If you conceive the color palettes as a progression through the sequence of spaces, the result will be a rich and dynamic layering of space, creating the impression of a larger, more spacious interior. In a compressed form, this layering is exactly how theater stage-set designers create the illusion of a vast space on a small stage.

In more fragmented interiors, where the rooms are separate from one another, the importance of harmonizing colors from room to room becomes less obvious. As you move from one space to the next, though, you will experience and remember the overall feel and tonality of each room. If you move from one space to another that is in sharp contrast to the previous one, you will sense the different personalities of each space, even if you can't literally distinguish or remember the exact color differences. So, if your goal is to give each space a distinct but related character, or if you are just trying to unify the interior, the interrelation of the palettes from space to space becomes important.

Ignoring the relationships between color palettes from room to room can create a disjoint feeling in the entire interior. Considering the palettes as a progression through a single, integrated composition leads to an environment that has unity and a sense of repose. People will often not be able to put their finger on why the interior feels so right, but they certainly will feel the effect and comment on it. Thinking in suites is not limited to interiors. When you look at your whole interior as a single composition, don't forget the exterior spaces and landscape beyond. The more connected an interior is to the landscape, the more valuable this approach becomes.

OPPOSITE | *The complementary colors of these two rooms create a layered effect. When the rooms are viewed as a suite, as in the photo, there is a greater sense of depth and interest in the overall interior.*

Existing Materials

Before starting with any color selections, survey all the existing permanent materials and features in the space, such as flooring materials, natural woodwork, tile, brick, art glass windows, or any other surfaces that have an integral color. If numerous materials and colors are present, you are starting off with a set of color relationships to which you must respond. Rather than thinking of this situation as a handicap, look at this preset palette as a jumping-off point. A common mistake is to ignore these colors if they don't necessarily fit your aesthetic vision. If you ignore them, they will not disappear—they will become disruptive accents that undermine the unity of the entire space. Often, even if some of the existing colors are not your favorites, there are ways to make transitions into your preferred colors. The more complex an existing palette is, the more ways there are to harmonize with it.

MAKING THE MOST OF DARK, NATURAL WOODWORK

Dark, natural woodwork in an interior presents specific color-design requirements. A frequent comment is: "The woodwork is so dark that I would like to make the rest of the space white to lighten up the room." The drawback of this approach is that a white backdrop for the dark woodwork makes the wood appear black and dull—the contrast is so great between the colors, and there is no related color to bring out the rich, warm undertones in the wood.

An alternative to this stark contrast is to look carefully at the warm tones in the wood and determine their color family. Even if the wood looks black or charcoal brown, other colors are usually mixed in, although they are sometimes subtle. If the wood tones include some orange, you might consider a soft peach for the walls, which allows you to keep the value of the room relatively light but will suddenly bring the wood to life. The woodwork will look richer, warmer, and more integrated into the space. The peach tone will also get rid of the choppy effect the dark woodwork creates against white walls.

ABOVE | *Dark Woodwork* The rich, russet wall color in this interior balances beautifully with the strong, dark woodwork. The warmth of the red picks up the otherwise subtle tones of red-brown in the woodwork and furniture. If this room were painted white instead of red, the woodwork would look heavy-handed and would chop up the space. The full, rich character of the architectural colors and textures in this interior create a simple but powerful design statement. This space could be furnished in many different ways, and it could be either cluttered or spare without losing its sense of order or warm sense of place.

ABOVE | *Many people have encountered one of these at one time or another—the bathroom with brightly colored and dated tile that you are forced to live with. Here, a multicolored scheme has been added that harmonizes with the tile. The tile now contributes to the whimsical color scheme, and the whole bathroom is transformed.*

TURN VISUAL IRRITANTS INTO ASSETS

If the space's existing colors seem disconnected and unharmonious, it is easy to select colors to act as a bridge. For example, a client brings me into an interior and tells me he is not at all fond of green and cannot tolerate the bright green tile around the fireplace. Adding to his displeasure, the antique art glass is full of bright gold colors, which appear brash and disconnected from anything in the room. In this instance, a solution might consist of a soft, creamy yellow for the walls, balanced with some accents of muted, grayed-down green. The cream color would tone down the gold in the art glass. The bright green tile now has some context with the addition of the gray-green bridge color. The overall tone and feel of the room is creamy yellow but is enlivened with the green and gold accents, which no longer look disconnected and jarring. A solution such as this transforms visual irritants into assets.

YOUR EXISTING FURNISHINGS AND BELONGINGS

Part of your existing context of materials includes the furnishings and belongings in your normal surroundings. Most frequently, it is neither practical nor desirable to start over with all new furnishings and objects each time you renovate an existing space or move to a new space. More often, your environment consists of a layered history of objects and furnishings. Some of these items might be important and valuable to you for various reasons, but often these collections of belongings do not necessarily have a visual or color cohesiveness. By creating a strong, clear, cohesive design statement in the integral architectural color, you can more easily weave the disparate personal items and furnishings harmoniously into your environment.

The advantage to this approach is that your space will truly be a reflection of who you are rather than looking like an impersonal model interior. The other advantage is that with strong integral architectural color, you can more easily add and delete things without disrupting the cohesiveness and harmony of the interior. Strong integral color also allows for more mess and process in your life. If the color and design success of your interior rely heavily on a certain set of carefully selected and placed objects, as soon as something is out of place or something is added, the cohesiveness is lost. In other words, life is messy—try to design for it rather than deny it. If you acknowledge and honor your own history and process in your environment, not only will your environment be a reflection and extension of you, but you will live in it more harmoniously.

COLOR HIERARCHY AND PROPORTIONS

The hues of the color wheel form a hierarchy, with some hues being naturally more dominant than others, even when used in precisely the same proportions. It is fairly easy to see which colors are dominant on the color wheel. As different values and chroma are introduced, the hierarchies become more complex. Changing the individual proportions of the selected colors also affects which color dominates. In other words, if a lot of any given color is present, it will be the dominant color. It is helpful to know which color will dominate in any given combination of colors. A few general principles to help guide you follow.

Dominant Hues

When viewed together, warm colors appear to advance while cool colors appear to recede. This is especially true when the different colors are viewed in similar proportions. The warmer colors actually trigger a different physiological response in the eye than the cool colors do—this is why the warm colors appear to be in the foreground. Warmer colors also elicit a stronger psychological reaction. Red, orange, and yellow are naturally more arousing and exciting than the more subdued and soothing blue, green, and purple.

Dominant Chroma

Purer colors advance and dominate while muted or grayed tones of the same color recede. Again, this rule assumes that the two colors appear in approximately equal proportions. Remember, the eye is naturally drawn to colors that are more intense.

It is helpful to know which color dominates so that it is not used in such a great quantity that it overpowers the other colors in the scheme. Understanding which color advances and which recedes can be useful if a greater apparent depth of space is desired. Intense colors can be used in the foreground with more subdued colors used in the background or recesses of a space. This placement creates a stage-set effect where recesses appear deeper than they actually are.

Figure 2.4 Primary red, yellow, and blue swatches of equal size show that the red advances and is dominant while the blue and yellow recede and are subordinate

Figure 2.5 Purer blue advances while the more muted, grayed blue recedes and is subordinate

ABOVE | *Dominant Hue* *The blue-green cabinets, the yellow walls, and the red beam in this kitchen are each of a similar intensity in color. Even though the red is the color used in the smallest amount, it is the first thing to which your eye is drawn. The red beam is the dominant hue in this space and creates a strong accent as it doubles as a pot rack.*

Dominant Values

Lighter values advance and dominate while darker values recede. This perception happens because more light is reflected off lighter-value colors, which makes them more luminous and draws the attention of the eye.

This principle can be applied to an interior to highlight the most important areas of the space. If an interior has medium to dark values and a few light accents, the eye will naturally be drawn to these lighter areas. Hence, it is important to be selective about what to highlight with lighter value accents.

Proportions of Color

As a general rule in designing colors for interiors, it is prudent to use the strongest or most dominant colors in the smallest amounts; otherwise, they tend to overpower the space and can become oppressive. When stronger colors are used in smaller amounts, they function as accents and serve to enliven the more muted or neutral colors. It is important to put the accent colors on elements to which you consciously want to draw attention.

Figure 2.6 The lighter value advances while the darker value recedes

LEFT | *Dominant Value* The wall colors in this suite of spaces are similar in hue. Your eye is drawn to the middle room because the lighter value of the green in this space has a more luminous quality. The changes in value from room to room create a rich layering of space in which each room has its own distinct character, but the progression from space to space is smooth and harmonious.

LEFT | *In this hallway, the brightest colors are used in the smallest amounts. The space remains clean, open, light, and spacious with the muted blue-greens and whites used to set the tone. The brightly colored furnishings then add rich accents without overpowering the space.*

RIGHT | ***Strongest Colors in Smallest Amounts*** *The warm colors and cool colors are carefully balanced in this child's room. The deeper accent colors are used in the smallest amounts, principally in the cornice/plate rail that rings the room. This cornice line organizes all the irregular shapes in the room by keeping a strong, clear, level dividing line between earth and sky, so to speak. An overglaze gives added depth to the accent colors in the cornice. The sky background consists of a graded wash of soft teal-gray, which gets lighter as it approaches the rising sun. The tiniest hint of gold leaf is applied around the sun's perimeter to provide a natural luminance. As the sun's light radiates outward, the colors make a gradual transition from warm back to the cool teal sky. When all these colors are combined into this single, unified composition, you actually can imagine yourself flying off into this picturesque sunrise.*

Figure 2.7 *Proportions of color as they appear in the child's room shown at right; note the strongest colors are used in the smallest amounts*

Figure 2.8 *Same colors as shown in Figure 2.7 but with proportions reversed; note how the entire feel and balance of the color scheme has been changed, even though the colors are exactly the same*

Tonality—Which Color Dominates?

As you have seen in the examples, at left, the relative proportions of colors can affect which color dominates. Generally, the color used in the greatest proportion in any color scheme defines the **tonality** of the scheme. The color that defines the tonality of the scheme is the **dominant** color. The next most prominent color would be the **subdominant** color, and the color that is used the least, or used as an accent, is called the **subordinate** color.

RIGHT | *Defining the Tonality* The burnt orange color in this interior dominates and sets the tonality. This red-orange color weaves the natural wood tones seamlessly into the entire space. The strong, cool blue accents keep the whole space from being heavy.

As can be seen in the photo on the right, even a strong gold color, which would ordinarily dominate, becomes subordinate when used in small amounts. As shown in the previous examples, the relative dominance of a color in a scheme is dependent on which colors are selected as well as on how much of each color is used.

Understanding the hierarchies of both the relative strength and the relative proportions of colors is important. This concept is essential to interior color design because an error in judgment becomes magnified when applied to a large area. Understanding and then effectively manipulating color hierarchies can produce outstanding results.

How Intense Should a Color Be?

A small color swatch, no matter how accurate, always ends up being deceptive. It is difficult to visualize the effect of a color in a large area when you select that color from a swatch measuring only a few square inches. The larger the area, the stronger a color appears. For example, what looked mostly gray with only a touch of lavender in a small chip can end up looking like a sickly purple when spread over an entire room. When in doubt, always opt for the more muted color, especially if there will be a lot of it.

To avoid this problem, always work from the largest color samples you can find. Whenever possible, test the color in a small area of the space. Always make sure that the sample color is viewed in the final location of the finished color. If it is a floor covering, view the sample on the floor. A ceiling color sample should be viewed on the ceiling. Each surface in the room receives a different amount and quality of light. As an experiment, hold a color sample on the ceiling and then place the same sample on the floor. For the most part, the sample on the ceiling will look considerably darker because there is less direct light. For this reason, it is better to err on the lighter side with color selections for the ceiling. It is also helpful to view the samples in both daylight and in whatever the source of artificial light will be.

ABOVE | *The warm tan walls dominate in this room, even though the deep gold accent band is a stronger color. Because the accent color is used in a small amount it becomes subordinate.*

HINT #3

The larger the area, the stronger a color will appear.

HINT #4

How to select colors from small sample swatches

The safest way to select a color from a relatively small sample swatch is to choose the color you prefer and then make the color less intense by lightening the value a step or two, or by graying the color a step or two.

Figure 2.9 *This yellow swatch in a small amount does not have much visual impact*

OPPOSITE | *The same yellow from the small swatch to the left has now been applied to an entire interior. Using the same color over a larger area radically amplifies the visual impact and perceived intensity of the color. The dramatically abstract, glowing yellow space creates a soaring stage set for this sculptural staircase.*

THE PSYCHOLOGY OF COLOR

The psychology of color is a rich and complex subject. It represents a field of study and research in and of itself. The psychology of color is also influenced by cultural and regional biases. There are, however, certain rules of thumb that can be used when attempting to predict and control the psychological effect a color might produce in an interior space. If you have any doubts, though, it is safest to test a color in your space before committing to it.

One important consideration is the position of the color in the space. The same color will appear very different on the floor versus on the wall versus on the ceiling. As an experiment, take a large swatch of color and hold it in each of these three different orientations. The starkest difference is the ceiling orientation, which makes the color appear grayer. The position of a color in the space also has a significant impact on the psychological effect of the color. For example, a rich burgundy carpet on the floor will feel warm, solid, and almost regal. That same burgundy on the ceiling will most likely look heavy, intrusive, and disturbing. So, orientation is a key consideration when you are trying to predict the psychological effect of a color selection.

Each color creates a relatively commonly shared set of psychological associations. These associations vary slightly from person to person, and they vary significantly depending on the context and surrounding colors. Still, it is helpful to have a set of general points of reference to better understand the psychological effect that each color creates.

ABOVE | *This Chinese red canopy bed creates a warm sense of enclosure and protection, especially in juxtaposition to the cooler green walls outside the enclosure. The red color advances, creating a sense of being wrapped in warmth.*

Common Color Associations

- **Red**—arousing, exciting, stimulating. It is also considered to be strong and masculine. It is a warm color and is often thought of as actually hot. It advances relative to other colors, making it appear closer. Red is associated with passion and vigor.
- **Pink**—soft, acquiescent, sensuous. As red shifts to pink, it often shifts gender association from masculine to feminine.

RIGHT | *The deep-red alcove creates a powerful sense of enclosure for the sofa. The strong color contributes to this commanding sense of closure more so than the actual shape of the space..*

RIGHT | *Even though the heavy classical architectural detailing of this bathroom has a masculine quality to it, the soft pink colors give the space a feminine balance.*

- **Orange**—exciting, stimulating, intense. The liveliness of orange has an almost whimsical quality that is less serious than red.
- **Peach**—soft, sunny, warm. Soft peach has a feminine quality to it.
- **Yellow**—luminous, sunny, cheerful. Soft yellows can seem expansive and open, which magnifies the feeling of spaciousness. Intense, pure yellows can seem acidic and irritating in large amounts but whimsical and energizing in smaller amounts.
- **Pale yellow**—neutral, expansive. As yellow pales, it loses its color and requires a cool adjacent color to react with to have any color dynamic in the space.

ABOVE | *The cheerful yellow kitchen feels as though it is bathed in luminous sunlight. The green brick backsplash creates a subtle focal point at the vintage range.*

ABOVE | *This classically detailed hallway is an interior space with no natural light. The warm peach color creates a soft, sunny quality where there is no actual sun.*

RIGHT | *This lively orange kitchen is chock-full of whimsically colored details. The colors are all in balanced harmony so that the whole effect is stimulating but very easy to live with.*

- **Green**—restful, relaxing, quiet. Deep greens can be somber by themselves but become fresh and full of life when contrasted against warmer colors. Pure greens have an association with vegetation.
- **Pale green**—lively when mixed with yellow. More quiet and introspective when mixed with blue.
- **Blue**—peaceful, calm, tranquil. Blue, when used in large amounts in its pure hues, can feel cool and melancholy.
- **Pale blue**—atmospheric, calm, spacious. Pale, cool blue tends to recede and, therefore, often makes spaces feel larger, especially when used on high ceilings.

LEFT | *The soft green tonality of this study creates a sense of quiet repose for someone who needs a calm environment in which to focus on tasks.*

ABOVE | *The quiet, calm blues on this porch invite you to relax in the rocking chair.*

- **Blue-green**—blue-green in its deeper forms is rich and complex. It spans the psychological associations of blue and green and often changes character with the changing light. Pale blue-green has a dense, atmospheric quality but does not recede as dramatically as pale blue.

- **Purple/Violet**—rich, regal, mystical. Purple has both a calm yet mysterious psychological association. Deeper purples and violets have a powerful yet introspective association.

- **Pale purple/Lavender** — soft, sensual, quiet. Pale purple and lavender often have a feminine association.

- **White**—purity, light, cleanliness. White has strong associations, even though we are often not fully aware of them. When used in excessive amounts, white feels sterile

- **Black**—power, elegance, dignity. Black also has strong psychological associations. When used in excessive amounts, black feels oppressive.

ABOVE | *The pale blue colors in this bedroom create a sense of atmospheric spaciousness even though the room is actually rather compact. The bright yellow and gold accents warm and enliven the space.*

ABOVE | The crisp, contemporary detailing in this dining room is balanced with the soft lavender and purples, which create a quiet and sensual dining environment.

ABOVE | The exquisitely detailed art glass and decorative furniture inlays are dramatically set off by their respective black frames. The color work in these ornate design features is vividly contrasted against the dark background, much the way jewels are set in a black velvet-lined jewelry box.

RIGHT | The multiple tones of white create a subtle layering in this living room. The gold and wood tones create balanced accents to add richness.

- **Gray**—conservative, quiet, calm. When mixed with quiet browns, gray can combine a warm richness with the sense of quiet dignity.
- **Brown**—earthy, stabile, secure. Brown is associated with the earth and natural materials. It often conveys a sense of permanence and familiarity.

ABOVE | *The deep earth tones combined with layers of history and patina give this living room a timeless sense of place and permanence.*

RIGHT | *This quiet gray living room conveys a sense conservative sophistication, which is enriched by well-balanced subtle brown and green accents.*

PERIOD INTERIORS

Knowing where to put color in a historical or period-style interior is as important as understanding how to design color combinations. A well-coordinated collection of colors is effective only if the colors are placed in the interior so that the right architectural elements are emphasized or deemphasized. Even a simple two-color scheme in a period interior can bring out the details of cornices, moldings, and columns.

Highlighting certain details can often help organize a room and give it scale. It can reduce the apparent ceiling height of a monumentally tall room, or it can simplify and unify a room that suffers from an excess of complicated detail.

ABOVE | *Classical Revival* The architectural detail is simple and spare in this interior, but the color placement brings out the design elements. The green accent on the ceiling highlights the elegant proportions of the curved rosette moldings. All the colors are subtle so the room retains a simple cohesiveness and allows flexibility in furnishings and decoration.

LEFT | *First Period* The colors are carefully selected to coordinate with the period woodwork and furnishings in this richly textured first-period dining room. The mustard-colored plaster with the subtle stencil patterns is a quiet accent for all the wood tones in the space.

Rules of Thumb for Color in Period Interiors

PROJECTIONS

- In any color scheme, the dominant colors and lighter values—or colors that advance—should be on those details that project out into the space. This will make projecting molding profiles, column capitals, and raised panels seem to have even more pronounced three-dimensional qualities and will add drama and character to the space.

RECESSES

- Subordinate colors and darker values—those that appear to recede—should be placed in recesses to emphasize the depth of the detail. This placement accentuates the natural shadow effect of the recesses. Avoid putting dominant colors in the recesses (and subordinate colors on the projections) because doing so tends to flatten the architectural detail instead of emphasizing its three-dimensional depth.

ABOVE | *Victorian Detail* The art glass and decorative window treatment are the focal points here. Note, however, that the architectural trim detail is called out in somewhat more subtle accents, so that these details play a supporting role in the overall composition.

LEFT | *Neo-Classical* The panel moldings and pilasters are subtly highlighted with a lighter value color so that the architectural detail is prominent enough to organize the room. The value difference between the colors of walls and trim is close enough that the room does not become choppy. The strongest colors are in the furnishings and objects.

KEEP IT SIMPLE

■ When in doubt, keep the overall color scheme simple and subdued. The goal is to highlight the architectural detail without overpowering it. Begin by accenting the details that are continuous around the room—such as cornice moldings, picture rails, and chair rails—to keep the accented lines continuous and simple. Avoid picking out each panel molding or door or window frame—this can break up the space and make it feel busy. If the panel moldings form a regular, rhythmic pattern as they march around the room, it may be safe to call them out with a subtle accent color.

LEFT | *Victorian* This highly decorated Victorian interior is typical of the period in that the decoration and color in the architecture and furnishings create a densely textured and patterned tapestry. One key to success in an interior such as this is to carry this tapestry-like texture throughout the space. Every surface is a candidate for decoration, from the floor all the way up to the ceiling surface itself.

ABOVE | *Arts and Crafts* Earth tones and natural materials are popular in Arts and Crafts interior palettes. This period kitchen features warm, mellow wood tones that play off multiple gradations of earthy green colors. Starting at the ceiling, the decorative stamped metal has a soft green wiped glaze. The backsplash tiles vary from light greens that harmonize with the ceiling to charcoal greens that meld into the adjacent woodwork. The counters are soft green and matte in finish. The spaces visible beyond the kitchen are a soft ochre color, which blends with the kitchen colors and is consistent with the period color palette.

RIGHT | *Early Twentieth Century* *This early-twentieth-century sitting area has an eclectic mix of architectural detail. The overall color palette is monochromatic but is filled with subtle variations in color to call out the many tiers of architectural detail. The stamped metal ceiling has a wiped glaze on it, which consists of a dark glaze applied over a lighter base color. When the glaze is wiped off, the darker color remains in the recesses and creates an even greater illusion of depth in the ceiling profile.*

CONTEMPORARY INTERIORS

There are many different types of contemporary interiors, and a few common rules of thumb can be applied to most contemporary spaces. To better understand color in contemporary interiors, it is helpful to identify some the fundamental differences difference between contemporary and traditional design.

The Design Intent

Try to understand the design intent of the space before deciding where to place the colors. Contemporary interiors are often composed of abstract, intersecting lines, planes, and volumes, which do not form neat little boxlike rooms or neatly framed and contained architectural detail. Play up the open-ended, interconnecting qualities of the space with the color placement. If some unifying design element is in the space, such as a soffit or other consistent design detail, it may be appropriate to subtly highlight it with color.

RIGHT | *Supporting the Architectural Design Intent with Color*

This living room brings the outdoors in. The exterior walls are white planking, which creates an association with traditional white clapboard houses and gives the impression of sitting on a porch. The sitting area rests on a warm wood floor that is completely surrounded by cool bluestone. The blue patina of exposed steel frames the space. The soft greens and purples of the sitting area float within the space and are bathed in natural light throughout the day. All of the material colors and applied colors in this contemporary space are in the service of the overall architectural design intent.

Planes and Volumes

If the interior is broken up into abstract planes and volumes, try treating each major plane or volume with a slightly different color. Effective color placement in such an interior can simplify and clarify the visual logic of the space. Without any color, this type of space can feel barren or chaotic. Often, it is most effective to use a low-contrast color scheme in a space such as this. Each color should be discernibly different from its neighbor without resorting to jarring contrasts.

Accent Elements

Accent colors can be used to draw attention to any special architectural features, such as railings, cabinetry, or millwork. It may be appropriate to employ stronger contrasts when selecting these accents; be sure that the particular architectural element selected is the proper one to highlight.

Color Trends

Color fashions and preferences tend to be cyclic in nature. Each cycle, color forecasters and fashion trendsetters tend to favor certain colors. Good color design is best achieved through inclusion of all available color choices. Otherwise, it is much like a composer excluding certain musical notes because they are not in fashion at that particular time. If you want to achieve the richest color design, choose from a full array of colors, but select the colors and compose the color relationships in careful response to the context and design goals.

ABOVE | *Volumetric Color* The deep blue tile in this bathroom creates the effect of a blue jewel box sandwiched between the sunny yellow bathroom and the warm glow of the outdoors beyond.

ABOVE *Natural Materials* The colors in this unusual bathroom are a careful balance between the cool colors of the natural stone complemented by the warm, natural wood tones. The green tub brings out the subtle greens in the stone.

LEFT | Volumetric Color The dynamic forms of this stairwell are expressed and clarified through the masterful use of color. The interior is composed of layers of abstract lines, planes, and volumes. Each element is expressed in either its natural material color or a harmonious paint color. The metal elements are the deepest colors and essentially form the bones of the space. The steel has a multicolored patina of blue, rust, black, and silver with a leatherlike character in places. The stainless steel cables, galvanized-steel window frames, and lead-coated copper soffit round out the palette of the metals.

Three distinct wood tones differentiate between stair, wall paneling, and wood framing visible in the space beyond. The space is then capped off with a series of abstract planes and volumes in soft greens and whites, which float ethereally above. As the sun's orientation changes, the natural light creates an ever-changing play of light and color.

Borrowed Color

A new frontier in color design is something I refer to as **borrowed color.** If a material or surface has no inherent color of its own but the color emanates from the complex interplay of reflected or diffused light on or through the material, the apparent color of the material is borrowed from its surroundings. The most prominent examples of borrowed color are found in the use of modern industrial materials. Frank Gehry's Guggenheim Museum in Bilboa, Spain, is the most famous example of borrowed color. The building is nearly entirely clad in titanium, a material rich in reflective qualities. The color of the actual material is a neutral gray-silver, but it never really appears neutral. As you change your viewpoint and as the day progresses, the light reflected off the titanium surfaces creates an ever-changing colored-light show that wanders through the entire spectrum.

In interior design, the reflective qualities of materials can be exploited in the same way to create borrowed color. Some other examples of borrowed color in interiors come from the translucency of architectural glass and industrial fabrics. Even ordinary, natural fabrics can be used to create unusual translucent color. Water, whether still or moving, is one of the oldest and time-honored ways of creating borrowed color.

The common thread in borrowed color is the interactive nature of the surrounding colors, materials, and ambient light. The resulting color effects are often more pleasing and satisfying because they are so dynamic. The color is dynamic in that it is ever-changing, at times subtle and other times dramatic. It is much more like the quality of light and color that we experience in nature. Think of the mutable colors of the ocean or the ever-shifting colors in the sky. These are universally appealing experiences of color and light. They connect us with the energy and power of light and color as a force of nature. Exploring the color qualities of light as it reflects off or passes through materials to create borrowed color is an area of design that is wide open for experimentation and invention.

ABOVE | *Virtually every surface in this kitchen is reflective, so the material colors interplay with reflected color and light throughout the space.*

ABOVE | *Reflected Color* The stainless steel trim around this tub does not have its own strong color. The steel reflects the subtle colors of the daylight spilling into the space and also picks up the warm colors of the adjacent materials. The result is a shimmering play of light and color, as if the tub were surrounded by a water feature instead of a cold piece of stainless steel.

LEFT | The unusual metal base on the coffee table glows with as much color and light as the fire in the fireplace beyond. The rich patina on the metal creates a combination of reflected color coupled with partitive color. Partitive color is created by mixing many small dots of different colors, which then appear to the eye as a single new color.

ABOVE | *Translucent Color* The bright colors in this sleeping alcove are flat, bold, and graphic. The glass panels above transmit a multifaceted, translucent green hue into the space. The complexity of the borrowed color coming through the glass panels is a balanced foil for the bold, flat colors below.

ABOVE | *Translucent, Layered Color* The sculptural details in this stair hall are decorated with subtle, translucent colors. This effect is achieved through the use of multiple overglazes and a finish of color-tinted varnish. Note the hint of green, rust, and mustard accents in the column capital and other moldings. These types of accents appear and disappear, like phantoms, with changes of light.

ABOVE | *Projected Color* The actual colors of the materials in this stair hall are quiet and subtle, yet the resulting qualities of color and light are rich and varied. The natural light cascades through the space and filters through the decorative railing cutouts. This creates a dappled effect of color and light, similar to the dappled light that spills through a canopy of tree foliage.

ABOVE | *Translucent Color* The golden light bathing this bedroom emanates from the warm, yellow translucent window shades.

LEFT | *Abstract Volume* This contemporary stairwell is composed of a careful balance of abstract planes and volumes. Each surface is called out in a softly contrasting color and texture so the composition forms a polychromatic sculpture bathed in natural light.

ABOVE | *Layered Color* Color is layered onto this interior much the way a fine arts painter layers colors in a watercolor painting. The difference is that because the forms are complex and three-dimensional, the reflected light enriches the depth of color. Note how the ceiling glows with reflected light from the burnt orange frieze. The decorative moldings are highlighted with green, rust, and mustard accents.

PRINCIPALS OF COLOR HARMONY

The most fundamental theory of color harmony in interior design is to ensure that the colors in any color scheme share some common traits or attributes. Remember that colors have three attributes:

- **Hue** or **Color**
- **Value** or **Lightness**
- **Chroma** or **Saturation**

Maintaining some similarities between colors ensures that they relate to each other and are, therefore, harmonious. Once a harmonious base color combination is established, add dramatic accents to enliven the color scheme and prevent it from being boring.

Similar Hue and Value

An easy way to achieve color harmony is to keep the hue and value the same while varying the chroma. Doing so means that the color scheme employs variations of a single color of a single relative lightness or darkness while varying the intensity of the color. Some of the colors might be more full bodied whereas others are more grayed down.

Similar Hue and Chroma

Another way to achieve color harmony is to keep the hue and chroma the same and vary the value. This type of scheme includes variations of the same color at the same intensity with only the relative lightness or darkness of the color changing.

Similar Value and Chroma

Yet another way to achieve color harmony is to keep the value and chroma the same and vary the hue. In this case, the relative lightness or darkness remains the same, as well as the saturation level of the color. Only the hue or actual color varies. Surprisingly, this last technique is often underutilized. By keeping the value and chroma constant and the colors slightly grayed (medium chroma), you can put together virtually any combination of colors to create extraordinarily complex schemes that are at the same time remarkably calm and harmonious.

ABOVE | *Similar Hue and Chroma* The colors in this kitchen vary only in value. Note the strongest color, on the ceiling, is used in the smallest amount.

HINT #5
Vary only one color attribute at a time.

LEFT | *Similar Hue and Value*

The colors in this cozy sitting room are similar in hue and value. The upper wall in the hallway is just a grayer version of the wainscot color. This effect creates a quiet color harmony.

ABOVE | *Similar Value and Chroma* *This richly colored bedroom incorporates three distinct and strong colors. Each color is of the same relative value and intensity, with only the actual hue varied.*

Chapter 3 Color Schemes and Examples

KEEPING IT SIMPLE

The simplest and safest color schemes to execute are the ones with just a couple closely allied colors. For some spaces, a monotone or monochromatic scheme is just the right approach. An example would be an interior where the contents and furnishings are very unified but interesting. Frequently, though, unless you acquire all your belongings with an eye for unified interior design, you will find yourself with a motley assortment of somewhat mismatched furniture and more belongings than seem to fit in a space. Your life will more often be filled with layers of belongings—an inherited desk, a special lamp from a trip to Europe, a quilt from your favorite aunt. To unify an eclectic assortment of furnishings and objects, it is essential to create a strong, but simple, architectural backdrop. Designers and decorators often refer to this as creating good bones for the interior.

MONOTONE SCHEMES

A monotone color scheme consists of various tints or shades of a single neutral color, such as gray, beige, or cream. This type of color scheme is a safe and conservative approach to interior color design. It is also effective when a variety of natural materials and textures are incorporated into the interior, because it allows these materials to take center stage.

Neutral Monotone Schemes

A neutral monotone color scheme is by far the most foolproof and conservative approach to decorating an interior. It allows the objects and artwork in the space to take the forefront by providing a simple, unobtrusive backdrop. A truly neutral, monotone color scheme is neither warm nor cool; rather, it is entirely neutral, as the description implies. It includes shades of white, off-white, and neutral grays and creates a serious and sophisticated ambiance in the space. Feelings evoked by this color design might include calm, businesslike, aloof, subtle, subdued, clean, austere, or stark.

LEFT | *Neutral Monotone* The quiet neutral colors in this interior create a sophisticated backdrop for the subtleties of the artwork and objects.

Cool Monotone Schemes

Cool monotone schemes might include green-grays, blue-grays, lavender-grays, or cool off-whites. A cool monotone interior tends to feel more airy, atmospheric, and light than a warm monotone interior. To avoid unpleasant starkness, furnishings can provide a few warm accents for balance.

Warm Monotone Schemes

Warm monotone schemes are also simple approaches to color design. Colors might include warm grays, beiges, and creams. The warm undertones of these colors can create an inviting, soothing, and cozy feeling. A strictly warm monotone interior benefits from a few cool accents in the form of artwork or furnishings.

ABOVE | *Cool Monotone* The tonality of this sitting space is cool in character. The carefully placed accent colors keep the room from feeling stark or barren.

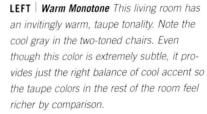

LEFT | *Warm Monotone* This living room has an invitingly warm, taupe tonality. Note the cool gray in the two-toned chairs. Even though this color is extremely subtle, it provides just the right balance of cool accent so the taupe colors in the rest of the room feel richer by comparison.

MONOCHROMATIC SCHEMES

Monochromatic color schemes consist of variations of a single color or hue. This kind of scheme can be dramatic, almost theatrical, in certain instances. A monochromatic color scheme is effective when your furnishings and belongings are consistent in color and character, and a single strong color will set the furnishings off as a unified composition. Monochromatic schemes should be used judiciously, though, because an interior done all in one color, especially a strong, deep one, can be overpowering. The safest approach to monochromatic schemes is to use medium to light values that are slightly grayed down.

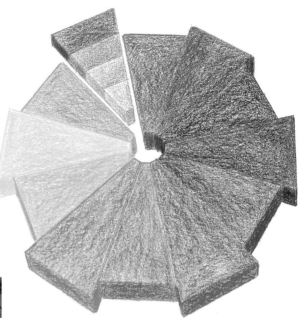

Figure 3.1 Monochromatic colors

LEFT | *Monochromatic* This entire bedroom is filled with variations on green. The wood tones and orange accents give the room balance without losing the effect of being enveloped in a garden of greens.

LEFT | *Monochromatic* *Even though this dining room has formal architectural details as a backdrop, the monochromatic violet color scheme with the lively accent colors give the space a lively sense of whimsy.*

ANALOGOUS SCHEMES

Analogous colors, or similar hues, are adjacent to each other on the color wheel. In subdued tints and shades, they can be harmonious. When selecting strong, more intense colors, an analogous color scheme is a reasonably safe approach to achieve color harmony. The general aesthetic and psychological effect of an analogous color scheme depends on the specific colors selected. Analogous schemes are relatively easy to execute and provide the flexibility to harmonize with a number of otherwise disparately colored furnishings. This type of scheme can be used as a problem solver for eclectic collections of belongings.

Figure 3.2 *Analogous colors*

LEFT | **Analogous** *The bold color statements in this living space are unified by the use of analogous colors to create color harmony. Green, blue-green, blue, and blue-purple are hues that are immediately adjacent to each other on the color wheel. The bright yellow accents add balance and interest.*

ABOVE | *Analogous* The oranges, yellows, and greens of this rustic interior form a close alliance on the color wheel. The wood tones tie into this color scheme seamlessly. Brightly colored Pez dispensers as fine art create an interesting and fun focal point.

COMPLEMENTARY SCHEMES

Complementary colors, or contrasting hues, are those found directly opposite each other on the color wheel. Complementary color schemes are often the most striking and lively yet the most difficult to execute well because a misjudgment in color selection can cause the scheme to be jarring. Study successful examples of complementary color schemes to understand what works and what doesn't. Designs using complementary colors are often described as exciting, cheerful, energetic, and vibrant.

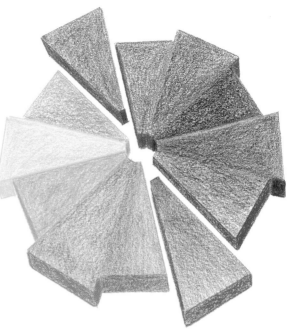

Figure 3.3 *Complementary colors*

LEFT | ***Complementary*** *The perfectly balanced complementary colors in this sitting alcove create a striking and sumptuous sanctuary. The red and green are similar in value and intensity; they differ from each other in hue only.*

BELOW | *Complementary* The yellow and purple accent colors on the walls of the dining room are complementary. Note the effect of the incandescent lighting on the colors. The warm color looks warmer and the cool color gets washed out.

Split Complementary

A split complement comprises one hue on one side of the color wheel and the two hues on either side of its complement. Split complements are always vibrant. It is important to tailor the strength of the scheme to be appropriate to the interior. When a split complement is executed skillfully, it is 'powerful and very effective.

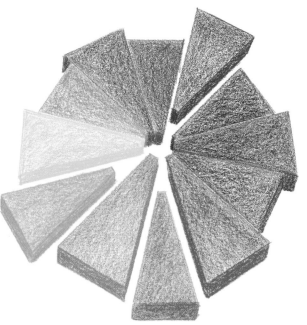

Figure 3.4 Split complements

LEFT | Split Complement The unusual color combination in this period dining area is an effective use of a split complement. The blue, raspberry, and gold colors are vibrant and unexpected but balance each other perfectly.

ABOVE | *Split Complement* Yellow-orange, red-orange, and blue are used effectively in a split complement palette in this cozy, contemporary interior.

RIGHT | *Split Complement* This graphic use of volumetric color is an example of a split complement used to create a boldly layered effect. The walls read as abstract planes and volumes.

Triads

A triad consists of any three equidistant colors on the color wheel. The primary colors—red, yellow, and blue—form the most common triad. Primary colors can be very stimulating in a child's environment because children respond to strong colors in their early stages of development. For an adult to live with nothing but primary colors for a long time could become tedious. When muted or lightened, triads can create rich, satisfying schemes that are more appealing to an adult's color sophistication.

Figure 3.5 Triads

LEFT | *Triad* The bright primary colors in this playroom are the most commonly used triad. Here, they are used in their full intensity to create a vibrant environment for children.

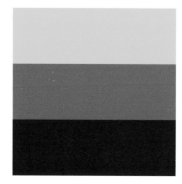

RIGHT | *Triad* The color palette in this living room is an example of a primary hue triad. The muted blue ceiling color is balanced against the burgundy red sofa. The yellow walls mediate between the two deeper colors.

Tetrads

A tetrad is any two pairs of complements. Tetrads are by far the most challenging to master in color design. Tetrads are often used in fabric, wallpaper, or other decorative arts where the colors can be interlaced together for balance and harmony. If you create a successful tetrad, the result will be a richly colored environment that offers tremendous latitude and flexibility for you to add other accent colors in the form of objects and furnishings.

Figure 3.6 *Tetrads*

LEFT | *Tetrad* *The vibrant colors in this dining room are well balanced. The yellow and orange oppose and balance the blue and purple, just as they balance on the color wheel.*

RIGHT | *Tetrad* This whimsical kitchen is full of color. The color relationships look like random fun, but the entire interior has a strong color harmony. The harmony is the result of the overall yellow-orange tonality accented with yellow-green, blue-purple, and purple-red. These color relationships form a perfect tetrad on the color wheel.

DISCORDANT COLORS FOR SPECIAL EFFECT

Sometimes, bending or breaking the rules of color harmony is useful and effective. So far, all of the color harmony principles discussed describe fairly symmetrical color balance. If you follow these principles rigorously, you will achieve harmonious combinations. However, perfect color harmony can sometimes be boring and predictable. A strong discordant color thrown into a scheme can make the design more dynamic.

Discordant colors can also be used to grab attention or to add an element of surprise. The important consideration is whether the color is drawing attention to the right thing at the right time. As a color designer gains knowledge and experience, the designs may become more adventurous.

RIGHT | *The consistent density of this unusual and inclusive mix of colors creates a collagelike environment.*

RIGHT | *This theme kitchen allowed the owners to take their fashion preferences to a new level. The attention to detail in this Burberry-inspired kitchen is all encompassing.*

Chapter 4 Step-by-Step Checklist

1 Consider Context

a. **Orientation of space and light**—north/south/east/west
b. **Proportions and shape of space**—what are the assets, and what are the design problems to solve?
c. **Think in suites**
d. **Consider existing materials**
e. **Consider existing furnishings and belongings**

2 Set Design Goals

a. **Set the emotional tone**—warm and cozy, cool and atmospheric, quiet and restful, vibrant and energetic, sensuous, serious, silly
b. **Focus color attention**—decide what to play up and what to play down
c. **Unify or identify**—determine if the space needs to be unified with one color or if it needs to be broken down into its individual design components and identified with different colors
d. **Warm or cool tonality**—decide if the tonality should be warm or cool; often dependent on orientation of the space

3 Preliminary Color Selection

a. **Select tonality**—decide which hue will dominate and set the tone of the space
b. **Select subordinate colors and accent colors**
c. **Check interaction of colors**—check the overall relationships of the dominant color, the subordinate colors, and the accent colors with all the existing colors in the space
d. **Adjust and tune**—adjust the colors until all the relationships look harmonious
e. **Check colors in the correct light and orientation**—check the color relationships in the light and orientation (floor, wall, ceiling) in which they will actually appear

Dominant Colors

a. **Dominant hues**—warm colors advance and dominate; cool colors recede and are subordinate

b. **Dominant chroma**—purer colors advance and dominate; muted colors recede and are subordinate

c. **Dominant values**—lighter values advance and dominate; darker values recede and are subordinate

Hints and Tips

HINT #1

Strong color relationships—not strong colors. Select the intensity of a color based on how it looks with the adjacent colors rather than how interesting it looks by itself.

HINT #2

Use the strongest color in the smallest amount.

HINT #3

The larger the area, the stronger the color will appear.

HINT #4

Selecting colors from small sample swatches. The safest way to select a color from a relatively small sample swatch is to choose the color you prefer and then make the color less intense by lightening the value a step or two, or by graying the color a step or two.

HINT #5

Vary only one color attribute at a time.

- Similar hue and value—keep hue and value similar and vary chroma
- Similar hue and chroma—keep hue and chroma similar and vary value
- Similar value and chroma—keep value and chroma similar and vary hue

Rely on your newly learned design tools…
but trust your intuition and…
above all, have fun.

PART II

COLOR SAMPLES

THE COLOR SAMPLES

Many different color palettes will work within a given space. Even within a given set of hues, there are many variations in color intensity and color values. The mood, color balance, and psychological feel within a space shifts in direct response to subtle variation in color. The dynamic range of color is truly limitless. Armed with some of the design tools outlined in this book, you will be ready to embark on your own color explorations.

The following examples are intended to spark your imagination and provide a starting point for your forays into color design. It would be impossible to show an example of every conceivable color scheme. The possible color combinations and effects are limited only by the skill and imagination of the designer. This chapter, however, covers all the basic color scheme categories. For each section, a sample color combination is shown in a sample interior that illustrates the flavor and character of the type of color combination being shown. Additional color combinations are then displayed in chip form. These other schemes could just as easily be substituted into the photo shown. Note that the chips are displayed in the relative proportions in which they appear in the interior. By showing the chips in the correct proportions, the combinations are a good indication of the tonality of the proposed scheme. This visualization tool should enable you to imagine and design many variations on a theme, either by copying the actual color chip combinations or, better yet, by inventing new variations. The color samples form a library of potential color schemes for ready reference. With all these tools, techniques, and points of reference, it should be possible to find your color voice and begin expressing your design ideas confidently in full, rich color.

MONOTONE
COOL MONOTONE

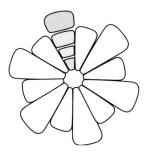

MONOTONE
WARM MONOTONE

MONOCHROMATIC
GREEN

MONOCHROMATIC
YELLOW-ORANGE

MONOCHROMATIC
BLUE

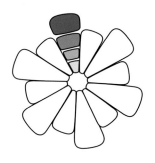

MONOCHROMATIC
YELLOW-GREEN

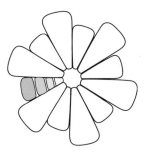

MONOCHROMATIC
YELLOW

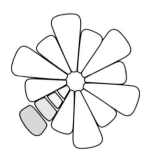

MONOCHROMATIC

YELLOW-ORANGE

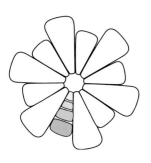

MONOCHROMATIC

ORANGE

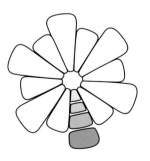

MONOCHROMATIC
BLUE-GREEN

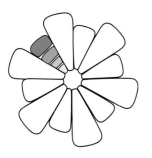

ANALOGOUS
GREEN, BLUE, BLUE-PURPLE

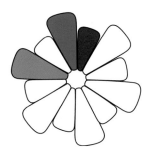

ANALOGOUS
YELLOW, GREEN, BLUE

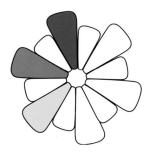

ANALOGOUS
YELLOW, GREEN, BLUE-GREEN

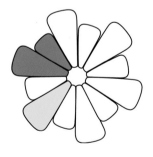

ANALOGOUS
GREEN, BLUE

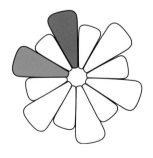

ANALOGOUS
YELLOW, GREEN, BLUE-GREEN

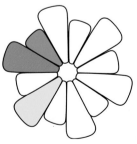

ANALOGOUS
GREEN, BLUE, PURPLE

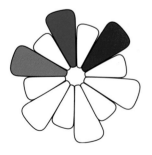

ANALOGOUS
YELLOW-GREEN, GREEN, BLUE-GREEN

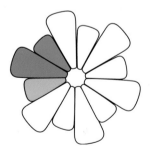

ANALOGOUS
PURPLE-RED, ORANGE-RED

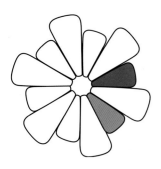

COMPLEMENTARY
ORANGE, BLUE

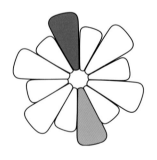

COMPLEMENTARY
ORANGE, BLUE

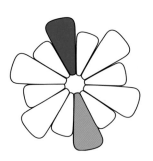

COMPLEMENTARY
YELLOW-ORANGE, BLUE-PURPLE

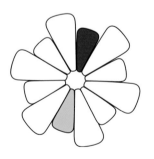

COMPLEMENTARY

GREEN, RED

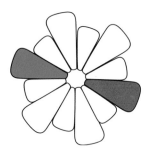

COMPLEMENTARY
BLUE-PURPLE, YELLOW-ORANGE

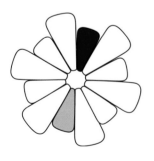

SPLIT COMPLEMENTARY
YELLOW, BLUE-PURPLE, PURPLE-RED

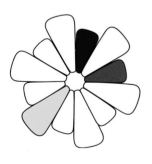

SPLIT COMPLEMENTARY
YELLOW-GREEN, BLUE, RED

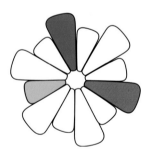

TRIAD
YELLOW, BLUE, RED

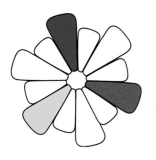

TETRAD

RED, ORANGE, BLUE, GREEN

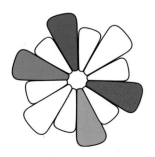

TETRAD

ORANGE-RED, YELLOW-ORANGE,
GREEN-BLUE, BLUE-PURPLE

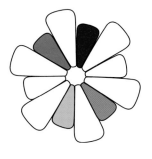

TETRAD
BLUE, PURPLE, ORANGE, YELLOW

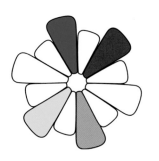

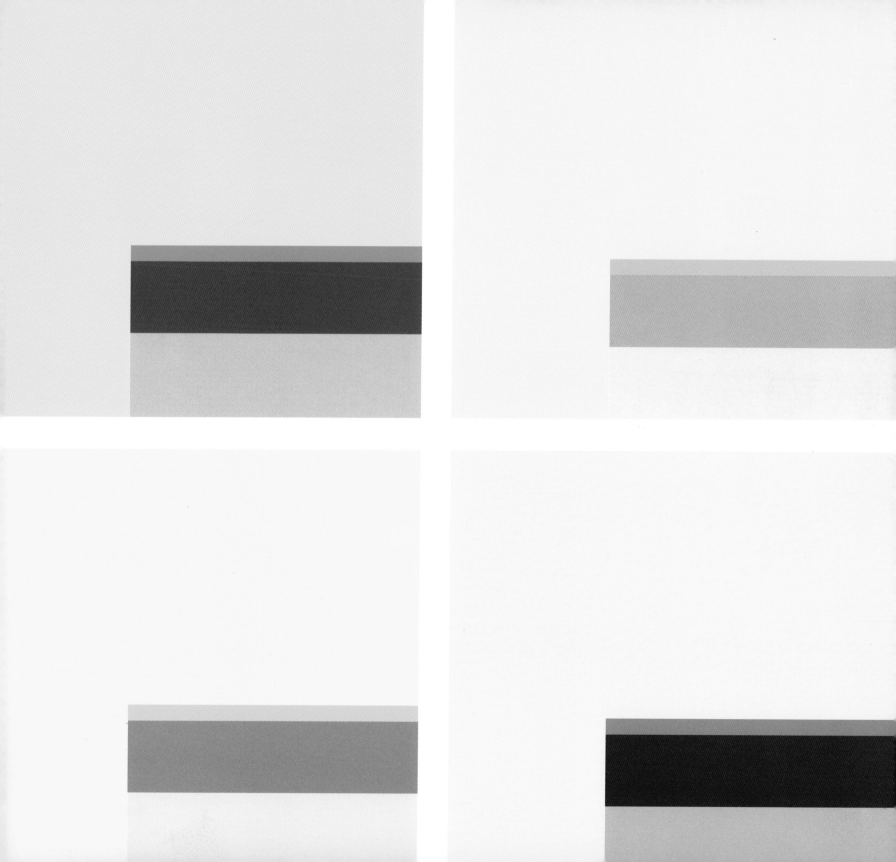

Glossary

Additive Color

Process of mixing colored light. The primary colors of red, green, and blue light make white light when mixed together.

Analogous Colors

Colors that are adjacent to each other on the color wheel.

Borrowed Color

Color achieved through the use of a reflective or translucent material that has little color of its own but borrows color from its surroundings.

Chroma

The relative strength or weakness of a color. Also called saturation.

Complementary Colors

Colors that are opposite each other on the color wheel, such as red and green.

Cool Colors

Blue-green, blue, and blue-purple are cool colors.

Hue

The name of a color.

Monochromatic

A monochromatic color scheme employs various tints and shades of a single color.

Monotone

A monotone or neutral color scheme consists of various tints and shades of a neutral color.

Neutral Color

A color that appears neither warm nor cool, such as gray.

Partitive Color

A color that is created by mixing many small dots of different colors, which then appear to the eye as a single new color.

Primary Colors

The primary colors of pigments and dyes are red, yellow, and blue. All other colors are derived from these three.

Saturation

See *Chroma*

Shade

A color created by adding black to a hue.

Split Complementary Colors

Colors made up of any color combined with the two colors on either side of its complement.

Subtractive Color

The process of mixing pigments, inks, or dyes. The primary subtractive colors are red, yellow, and blue, from which all other colors are derived.

Tetrad

Any two pairs of complementary colors.

Tint

A color created by adding white to a hue.

Tone

A color created by adding gray to a hue.

Tonality

The overall impression made by the dominant color in a color scheme.

Triad

Any three equidistant colors on the color wheel. The primary colors, red, yellow, and blue, form a triad.

Value

The relative lightness or darkness of a color.

Warm Color

Red, orange, and yellow are warm colors.

Bibliography

Albers, Joseph. *Interaction of Color.* New Haven: Yale University Press, 1963.

Amos, Gwen. "Color Theory in Practice." *Step by Step Graphics 7,* No. 2 (March/April 1991): 74–83.

Birren, Faber. *Color and Human Response.* New York: Van Nostrand Reinhold, 1978.

Eckstein, Helene. "Understanding Basic Color Concepts." *Step by Step Graphics 7,* No. 2 (March/April 1991): 62–69.

Eiseman, Leatrice, and Lawrence Herbert. *The Pantone Book of Color.* New York: Harry N. Abrams, Inc., 1990.

Faulkner, Waldron. *Architecture and Color.* New York: Wiley-Interscience, 1972.

Fishel, Catharine. "The Psychology of Color." *Step by Step Graphics 7,* No. 2 (March/April 1991): 84–91.

Gage, John. *Color and Culture.* Berkeley and Los Angeles: University of California Press, 1993.

Gage, John. *Color and Meaning.* Berkeley and Los Angeles: University of California Press, 1999.

Gerstner, Karl. *The Forms of Color: The Interaction of Visual Elements.* Cambridge: MIT Press, 1986.

Itten, Johannes. *The Color Star.* New York: Van Nostrand Reinhold, 1985.

Lena, Nicholas M. "Light and Color Evaluation." *Step by Step Graphics 7,* No. 2 (March/April 1991): 70–73.

Mahnke, Frank H. *Color, Environment, and Human Response.* New York: John Wiley and Sons, Inc. 1996.

Munsell, A. H. *A Color Notation.* Baltimore: Macbeth, a Division of Kollmorgen Corporation, 1981.

Pentak, Stephen, and Richard Roth. *Color Basics.* Belmont, CA.: Wadsworth/Thomson Learning, 2004.

Zelanski, Paul, and Mary Pat Fisher. *Color.* Upper Saddle River, NJ: Prentice-Hall, 2003.

Designer Credits

Page 136
Jon Andersen Design
617-536-0004

Page 56 (right)
Chris Benson
617-536-0285

Page 30 (right)
Beauport
The Sleeper-McCann House
Gloucester, Massachusetts 01930
978-283-0800
www.historicnewengland.org

Page 15
Marty Braun

Page 65; 67 (top left)
Gregor D. Cann
CannDesign
www.canndesign.net
866-350-CANN

Page 84
Circle Furniture
www.circlefurniture.com

Page 4; 40; 47; 77
Clancy Cottage

Page 25 (bottom); 64 (top)
Dennis Duffy
www.duffydesigngroup.com

Page 122; 142; 150
Anne Fitzgerald

Page 62
Chris Gustin
www.gustinceramics.com

Page 31; 58 (left)
Jon Hattaway
M.J. Berries
617-357-5055

Page 57 (right)
Ned Jalbert Design
508-836-9999

Page 78
C & J Katz Design
617-464-0330

Page 82
Julie Knisley
June Bug Rockers
www.coolchair.com

Front cover (bottom); 12; 41; 79; 81
(bottom); 116
Tacey Luongo
Renny Corporation
617-569-6405

Page 130
Chad Mize

Page 39 (right); 81 (top); 112;
114; 140
Adolfo Perez
www.adolfoperez.com

Page 70
Polly Peters Design
207-774-6981

Page 24 (right); 26; 27 (right); 28; 36
(left); 37; 38; 46; 48; 53 (right); 59
(right); 60; 66 (left); 67 (right); 68;
69 (left); 83; 88; 100; 102; 144; 160
Jonathan Poore

Page 52 (top right)
Louis Postel
617-499-1992

Page 73; 96
Frank Roop Interior Design
www.frankroop.com

Page 61; 63 (left); 67 (bottom left);
132
Architect: James Rowe
Agoos/Lovera Architects
Agooslovera.com

Front cover (top); 7; 10; 21; 45; 76;
98; 120; 124; 148
Susan Sargent
www.susansargent.com

Page 11
Judy Schultze
502-245-0560

Page 138
Judy Schwartze
502-245-0560

Page 54; 55 (bottom right); 72
Charles Spada
617-951-0008

Page 65 (bottom right)
David Tonnesen
www.dtonnesen.com

Page 51 (top right)
Douglas Truesdale
617-695-3800

Page 66 (right)
Gary Wolf Architect
617-742-7557

Page 56 (top left); 57 (left); 152
Harry Zeltzer
The Baker Sutton House Antiques
978-356-0447

About the Author

Laurel McDonald

Jonathan Poore is an architectural designer, illustrator, and writer. His work has appeared in *The Journal of Light Construction, The Naturally Elegant Home* by Janet Marinelli (Little, Brown), the *New York Times, Old-House Journal, Progressive Architecture,* and other publications. He has a design and consulting business that provides comprehensive integrated design services. This interdisciplinary design approach includes detailed site, landscape, architectural, interior, lighting, and color design. Most of his projects combine all these design facets into one cohesive whole, but he also offers each of these services, including color consulting, as independent tasks. He has a broad background in historic preservation and has served as chairperson for his local historic district commission for over fifteen years. His study of historic architecture and the associated decorative arts has deepened his appreciation for the power of color in design. Jonathan lives on the north shore of Massachusetts with his wife and two children.

About the Photographer

Sabrina Murphy

Photographer Eric Roth is now more enthusiastic than ever about his work. The variety of homes and how people live fascinates him, as does photographing them for books and magazines. His work is published in numerous titles, including *Country Interiors*, *New Country Colors*, *New England Style*, *Garage*, *East Coast Rooms*, *The Inspired Workspace*, *Eclectic Rooms*, *The Comfortable Home*, *House Beautiful Bedrooms*, *Small Homes*, and *Modern Nostalgia*. He is also a regular contributor to various magazines, such as *Yankee*, *Elle Décor*, *Home*, *Traditional Home*, the *Boston Globe Magazine*, *Old-House Interiors*, *House Beautiful*, *Boston Magazine*, and *Cape Cod Home & Garden*. Other book projects, *The Pubs of Ireland*, *The Turkish Baths of Istanbul*, and *The Art of Interior Photography*, are in production. He shares a home north of Boston with Becky, his wife of 29 years, and his daughters, Madeline and Charlotte.

Photo credit: Laurel McDonald

Acknowledgments

I wish to thank Christina Ward, my agent, for her encouragement and assistance in making this book project possible. I would like to credit Mary Ann Hall and Betsy Gammons, my editors, for all their guidance and help in keeping the process moving smoothly. Special thanks go to Eric Roth for his keen eye and fine photography. I would like to express my appreciation to Sabrina Murphy, Eric's assistant, who provided invaluable assistance in gathering and organizing the photographic images for this book. Thanks also to my loyal office staff and their unquestioning assistance during deadlines. And finally thanks to my wife Sharon, for her editorial wisdom, as well as her patience and support.

–Jonathan Poore

Hard work would be unfulfilling without people to do it with, and to do it for.

I am very lucky to have people who have helped and inspired me. I carry their spirit with each new endeavor.

Thanks to Sabrina Murphy, Betsy Gammons, Russ Mezikofsky, Estelle Bond Guralnick, Gail Ravgiala, Susan Sargent, Charles Spada, Leslie Wagner, Victoria Craven, James Baker Hall, Brian Swift, Paul Yandoli, Joe Picard, Frank Braman, Dan Cutrona, Suzy Makepeace, Janet and Dave Henderson, Ivan Orlicky, Ellen Rogers, and my loving parents, Bernie and Phyllis Roth.

–Eric Roth